Animal Migrations

Deer and Antelope Migration

by Susan Johnston Taylor

FOCUS
READERS.

BEACON

www.focusreaders.com

Focus Readers is distributed by North Star Editions:
sales@northstareditions.com | 888-417-0195

Produced for Focus Readers by Red Line Editorial.

Photographs ©: Shutterstock Images, cover, 1, 4, 7, 8, 11; iStockphoto, 13, 14, 17, 19, 20–21, 22, 25, 27, 29

Library of Congress Cataloging-in-Publication Data
Names: Johnston Taylor, Susan, author.
Title: Deer and antelope migration / by Susan Johnston Taylor.
Description: Lake Elmo, MN : Focus Readers, [2024] | Series: Animal
    migrations | Includes index. | Audience: Grades 2-3
Identifiers: LCCN 2022060036 (print) | LCCN 2022060037 (ebook) | ISBN
    9781637396063 (hardcover) | ISBN 9781637396636 (paperback) | ISBN
    9781637397749 (pdf) | ISBN 9781637397206 (ebook)
Subjects: LCSH: Deer--Migration--Juvenile literature. |
    Antelopes--Migration--Juvenile literature. | Deer--Behavior--Juvenile
    literature. | Antelopes--Behavior--Juvenile literature.
Classification: LCC QL737.U55 J65 2024 (print) | LCC QL737.U55 (ebook) |
    DDC 599.64--dc23/eng/20230117
LC record available at https://lccn.loc.gov/2022060036
LC ebook record available at https://lccn.loc.gov/2022060037

Printed in the United States of America
Mankato, MN
082023

About the Author

Susan Johnston Taylor is the author of *Animals in Surprising Shades: Poems About Earth's Colorful Creatures* (Gnome Road Publishing, 2023). Her poetry also appears in *10.10 Poetry Anthology: Celebrating 10 in 10 Different Ways*. She's written more than a dozen titles for the educational market.

Table of Contents

Chapter 1

Mule Deer on the Move

A family of mule deer scurry across Wyoming's Red Desert. Their fur blends in with the land. Dusk comes to the desert, cooling the spring air. The deer nibble on grass.

Mule deer live for approximately 10 years in the wild.

The next morning, their trip continues. Days pass. The deer travel hundreds of miles. They cross rivers and highways. They slide under fences.

Finally, the deer reach their summer **range** in eastern Idaho. They spend the warmest months

Fun Fact

In the winter, mule deer form bigger **herds**. These large groups help the deer stay safe.

 Mule deer stop at a river during their migration.

there. They munch on plants.
Females give birth.

In the fall, the air gets colder. The mule deer return to their winter range. This cycle repeats year after year.

Chapter 2

Why Migrate?

Some animals live in places that don't get too hot or too cold. The animals can usually find food all year long. So, they don't need to move very far. These animals are called residents.

 Many white-tailed deer stay in the same area their whole lives.

Other animals need to **migrate**. Moving helps them find food. It also helps them avoid harsh winters. Many deer and antelope migrate. They travel south for the winter. Then they move north for the summer.

Deer and antelope are related. But they have a few differences. Male deer lose their antlers each winter. They grow new antlers each spring. Most female deer don't grow antlers. In contrast, male antelope

 Some deer herds have taken the same routes for hundreds of years.

grow horns. Some female antelope also grow horns. Unlike deer, antelope do not shed their horns.

There are several types of deer. Moose are the largest. They live in cold places such as Canada and Alaska. Elk are another large deer. Some elk live in the western United States and Canada. Others live in Asia. Caribou are deer as well. They live in North America, Europe, and Asia.

Fun Fact

In the spring, deer migrate to areas where plants are starting to grow. This is called green-wave surfing.

Moose can weigh up to 1,500 pounds (680 kg).

There are also several types of antelope. Gazelles live in Africa and Asia. Wildebeests live in southeast Africa. Pronghorn are not a type of antelope. But they look very similar. Pronghorn live in North America.

Chapter 3

Migration Routes

Caribou travel far. Their migration is the longest of all land animals in North America. One large herd spends the spring in northern Alaska. The caribou find plenty of food in this area.

 Outside North America, caribou are known as reindeer.

Females give birth there, too. The area doesn't have many **predators**. So, the **calves** stay safe. However, food starts to run low in the fall. So, the herd moves south. Calves can walk up to 10 miles (16 km) every day. During winter, snow covers the ground. The caribou use their hooves to dig for food.

Moose don't migrate as far as caribou. Moose tend to stay near lakes or **wetlands**. They are good swimmers. Some moose

 Swimming helps moose stay cool during warm weather.

swim between islands during the summer. They can even close their **nostrils** underwater. Moose also have good hearing. And they have a strong sense of smell. This helps them stay safe from predators.

Mongolian gazelles migrate long distances across Asia. During the summer months, their coats are reddish-yellow. But their coats lighten during winter. This helps gazelles blend in with the **environment**. That way, predators are less likely to see them.

Fun Fact

Wildebeests cross many rivers during their migration. Sometimes crocodiles attack them.

 Wildebeests are also called gnus.

Wildebeests make a huge loop across southeast Africa each year. The route is based on rain patterns. Rain helps grass grow. Wildebeests often go where rain has fallen to find food.

Caribou Herds

Caribou can walk 2,000 miles (3,200 km) in one year. They move in large herds. The Western Arctic Herd (WAH) is in Alaska. It has hundreds of thousands of caribou. The WAH is one of the largest caribou herds in the world.

During the summer, caribou form tight groups. These are called aggregations. The caribou in each group stay close together. Their bodies touch. This helps them avoid mosquitoes. That's because there is less space for the mosquitoes to bite.

During winter, caribou eat plant-like organisms called lichens.

Chapter 4

Dangers Along the Way

Migrating deer and antelope face many dangers. For example, they may get hurt crossing rivers. Or predators may eat them. However, the biggest danger is humans.

 Fast-moving cars are a threat to many migrating deer and antelope.

Humans put up fences, buildings, and roads. All these things can block animals' paths.

Wyoming has large areas where people drill for gas. These gas fields are in mule deer's winter range. So, the deer changed their migration path. They avoided these areas. But now the deer have less space than before. Scientists worry this will lead to fewer deer in the future.

Antelope are in trouble, too. Addax antelope migrate in small

 Addax live in the Sahara Desert. As of 2023, fewer than 500 addax were left in the wild.

groups. They are endangered. Hunters have killed many of them. Very few are left in the wild. Addax are an important food source for other animals. They also keep soil healthy by **grazing** on grass.

Scientists want to keep deer and antelope safe. So, they study the animals' migration. Tracks and poop offer clues. They help scientists guess how many deer or antelope are in an area.

Scientists also attach collars to animals. These collars send out

Fun Fact

Some places have animal crossings by highways. Tunnels or bridges help animals cross the road safely.

 Animal crossings give deer a safe path across highways and railroads.

radio waves. That way, scientists know where the animals are. This information helps them map migration paths. Learning where animals travel helps scientists do more to protect them.

FOCUS ON

Deer and Antelope Migration

Write your answers on a separate piece of paper.

1. Write a sentence that describes the main ideas of Chapter 2.

2. Do you think scientists are doing enough to help deer and antelope? Why or why not?

3. Which type of deer has the longest migration?
    - **A.** mule deer
    - **B.** moose
    - **C.** caribou

4. If humans block a deer's migration path, what problem could happen?
    - **A.** Deer won't reach places with enough food.
    - **B.** Deer will have too many babies.
    - **C.** Deer will stop blending in with their environment.

5. What does **residents** mean in this book?

*So, they don't need to move very far. These animals are called **residents**.*

    A. animals that sleep under logs or rocks
    B. animals that live in the same place
        all year
    C. animals that are active only at night

6. What does **endangered** mean in this book?

*Addax antelope migrate in small groups. They are **endangered**. Hunters have killed many of them. Very few are left in the wild.*

    A. a common source of meat
    B. able to fight bigger animals
    C. in danger of dying out

Answer key on page 32.

Glossary

calves
The young of certain animals such as antelope and large deer.

environment
The natural surroundings of living things in a particular place.

grazing
Eating small bits of food throughout the day.

herds
Groups of animals that stay together.

migrate
To move from one region to another.

nostrils
Openings in the nose that are used for breathing.

predators
Animals that hunt other animals for food.

range
The area where a certain kind of animal naturally lives.

wetlands
Areas of land that have a lot of moisture, such as marshes or swamps.

To Learn More

BOOKS

Donnelly, Rebecca. *On the Move with Caribou*. Minneapolis: Jump!, 2023.

London, Martha. *Saving Caribou*. Lake Elmo, MN: Focus Readers, 2021.

Murray, Julie. *Deer*. Minneapolis: Abdo Publishing, 2020.

NOTE TO EDUCATORS

Visit **www.focusreaders.com** to find lesson plans, activities, links, and other resources related to this title.

Index

Answer Key: 1. Answers will vary; 2. Answers will vary; 3. C; 4. A; 5. B; 6. C